A DAREDEVIL'S GUIDE TO Swimming with SHARKS

by Amie Jane Leavitt

Consultant:
Gregory Skomal, PhD
Massachusetts Marine Fisheries
New Bedford, Massachusetts

CAPSTONE PRESS
a capstone imprint

Velocity Books are published by Capstone Press,
1710 Roe Crest Drive, North Mankato, Minnesota 56003
www.capstonepub.com

Library of Congress Cataloging-in-Publication Data
Leavitt, Amie Jane.
A daredevil's guide to swimming with sharks / by Amie Jane Leavitt.
p. cm. — (Velocity. Daredevils' guides)
Includes bibliographical references and index.
Summary: "Describes swimming with sharks for scientific study and as part of a tour group, the dangers involved, the gear needed, and what scientists have learned from their quests"—Provided by publisher.
ISBN 978-1-4296-9985-3 (library binding)
ISBN 978-1-4765-1806-0 (ebook PDF)
1. Sharks—Juvenile literature. 2. Sharks—Research—Juvenile literature. I. Title.
QL638.9.L396 2013
597.3'3—dc23 2012020517

Editorial Credits
Carrie Braulick Sheely, editor; Veronica Scott, designer; Wanda Winch, media researcher; Laura Manthe, production specialist

Photo Credits
Corbis: Jeffrey L. Rotman, 14, 34-35, 36-37, National Geographic Society/Mauricio Handler, 26-27, Science Faction/Scubazoo - Roger Munns, 30; Digital Stock (Corbis), 25 (top), 41(bottom); Dreamstime: Fiona Ayerst, 12 (bottom left), Willtu, 10-11; Getty Images Inc: Photographer's Choice/Jeffrey L. Rotman, 4-5; iStockphotos Inc: Turnervisual, 12-13 (back); Jon Hughes, 8-9; Newscom: EPA/Boston Globe/Wendy Maeda, 31, Photoshot/Evolve/Linda Pitkin, 32, Zuma Press/A-Frame/Nevins, 13 (t), Zuma Press/Vwpics/Andy Murch, 41(t); Robert S. Dietz Museum of Geology, Arizona State University/Brad Archer, 9 (b), Shark-Free Marinas.com, 43; Shutterstock: A Cotton Photo, 6 (b), Anton Balazh, 33, brandelet, cover (back), 40-41 (back), Dray van Beeck, 7 (m), Eky Studio, 8-9 (back), 32-33 (back), Emelyanov, 30-31 (back), Excellent Backgrounds, 14-15 (back), FAUP, 11 (b), 12 (br), frantisekhojdysz, cover (br), 44 (b), Greg Amptman's Underseas Discoveries, 18-19, 20-21 (back), 22, 24-25, 44-45, Jim Agronick, 6 (t), 13 (br), 15, Krzysztof Odziomek, 7 (t), Lauren Cameo, 16-17, leonello calvetti, 6-7 (back), Linda Bucklin, cover (m), 1, Mark Doherty, 7 (b), Nastya Prieva, cover (tr), Nataliia Natykach, 22-23 (back), Photocreo Michael Bednarek, cover (tl), prudkov, blur background, Rain Returns, 36-37 (back), Rich Carey, 38-39, Stephen Marques, 20-21 (map), Stephen Nash, 42, vic927, cover (back), Willyam Bradberry, cover (t); SuperStock Inc: Minden Pictures, 28-29

Printed in the United States of America in Stevens Point, Wisconsin.
092012 006937WZS13

Table of Contents

IT'S A SHARK!

A speedboat loaded with tour group members jets toward a Tahitian island. But this is no ordinary sightseeing tour. In minutes, the passengers will be face to face with huge, toothy sharks. The speedboat glides to a stop. The boat captain calls the attention of everyone on board. "We will start our shark feeding tour in a few minutes," he announces. "Before you get into the water, though, we'd like you to look over this side of the boat," he says, pointing to his right. A rope stretched out from the boat to a small buoy floating in the water. "This is the shark danger zone. Whatever you do," he warns, "do not go on this side of the rope."

After putting on their masks and snorkels, the passengers hop off the side of the boat. Everyone is on the proper side except for one man. He hadn't been paying attention and had jumped in on the wrong side of the rope.

"What are you doing?" the boat captain shouts. "Move quickly to the other side," he says, flailing his arms in panicky motions.

The man in the water is so startled that he looks as though his eyes will pop out of his head. He can only imagine the danger he has placed himself in. He instantly starts swimming frantically to the other side of the rope. Once on the other side, he clasps the rope firmly and tries to slow his breathing. He is safe at last.

The captain and his assistant then dive into the "danger zone" on the opposite side of the rope as the passengers. They toss small pieces of food into the water. Some tour members bob up and down while holding desperately to the rope. They try not to drift to the other side. Others hold on, too, but they also look into the water to see if sharks are underneath them.

"The very first time I stuck my head in the water," an attendee explains after the tour, "I saw a shark swimming right for me! His eyes were a pale blue and his skin looked like gray silk. As soon as I saw him, my heart started pounding and I gasped for breath. I grabbed my friend's shoulder and spouted a muffled yell through my snorkel, 'Oh my goodness! It's a shark!'" She smiles brightly showing a picture of the shark on her camera screen.

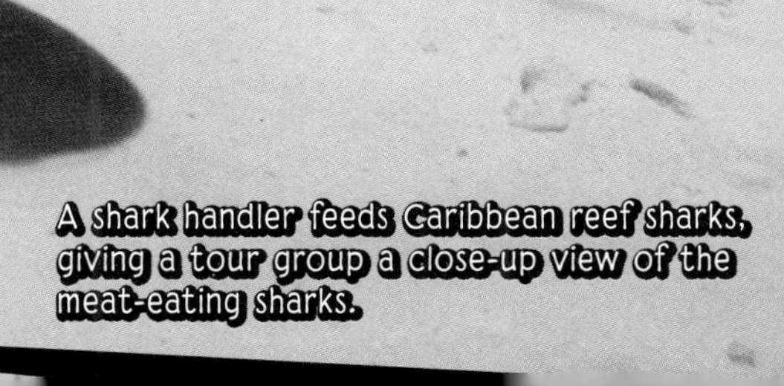

A shark handler feeds Caribbean reef sharks, giving a tour group a close-up view of the meat-eating sharks.

Chapter 1

HUNDREDS OF SPECIES

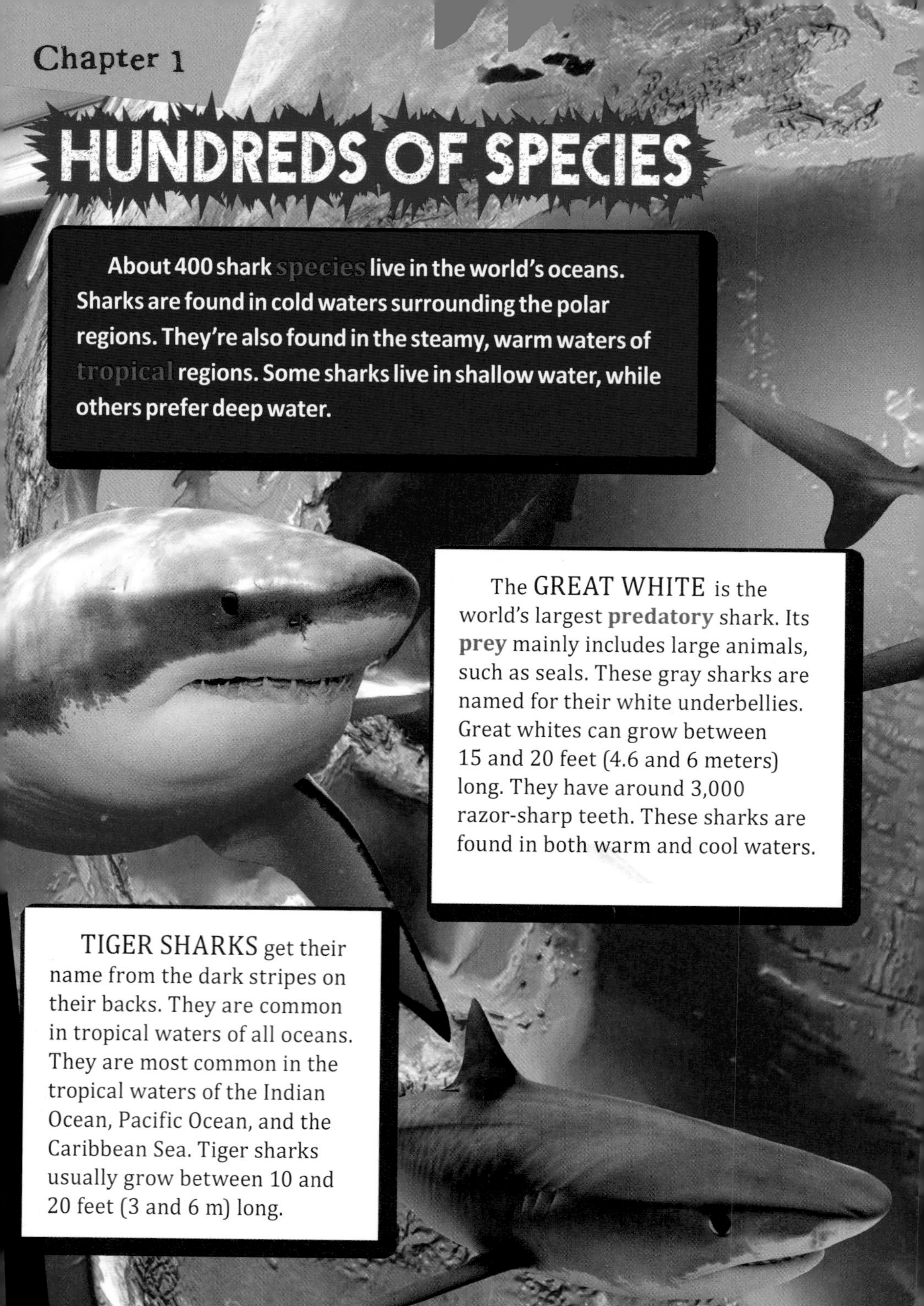

About 400 shark species live in the world's oceans. Sharks are found in cold waters surrounding the polar regions. They're also found in the steamy, warm waters of tropical regions. Some sharks live in shallow water, while others prefer deep water.

The GREAT WHITE is the world's largest **predatory** shark. Its **prey** mainly includes large animals, such as seals. These gray sharks are named for their white underbellies. Great whites can grow between 15 and 20 feet (4.6 and 6 meters) long. They have around 3,000 razor-sharp teeth. These sharks are found in both warm and cool waters.

TIGER SHARKS get their name from the dark stripes on their backs. They are common in tropical waters of all oceans. They are most common in the tropical waters of the Indian Ocean, Pacific Ocean, and the Caribbean Sea. Tiger sharks usually grow between 10 and 20 feet (3 and 6 m) long.

species—a group of animals or plants that share common characteristics

tropical—having to do with the hot and wet areas near the equator; the equator is an imaginary line around Earth's middle that divides the planet into a northern half and a southern half

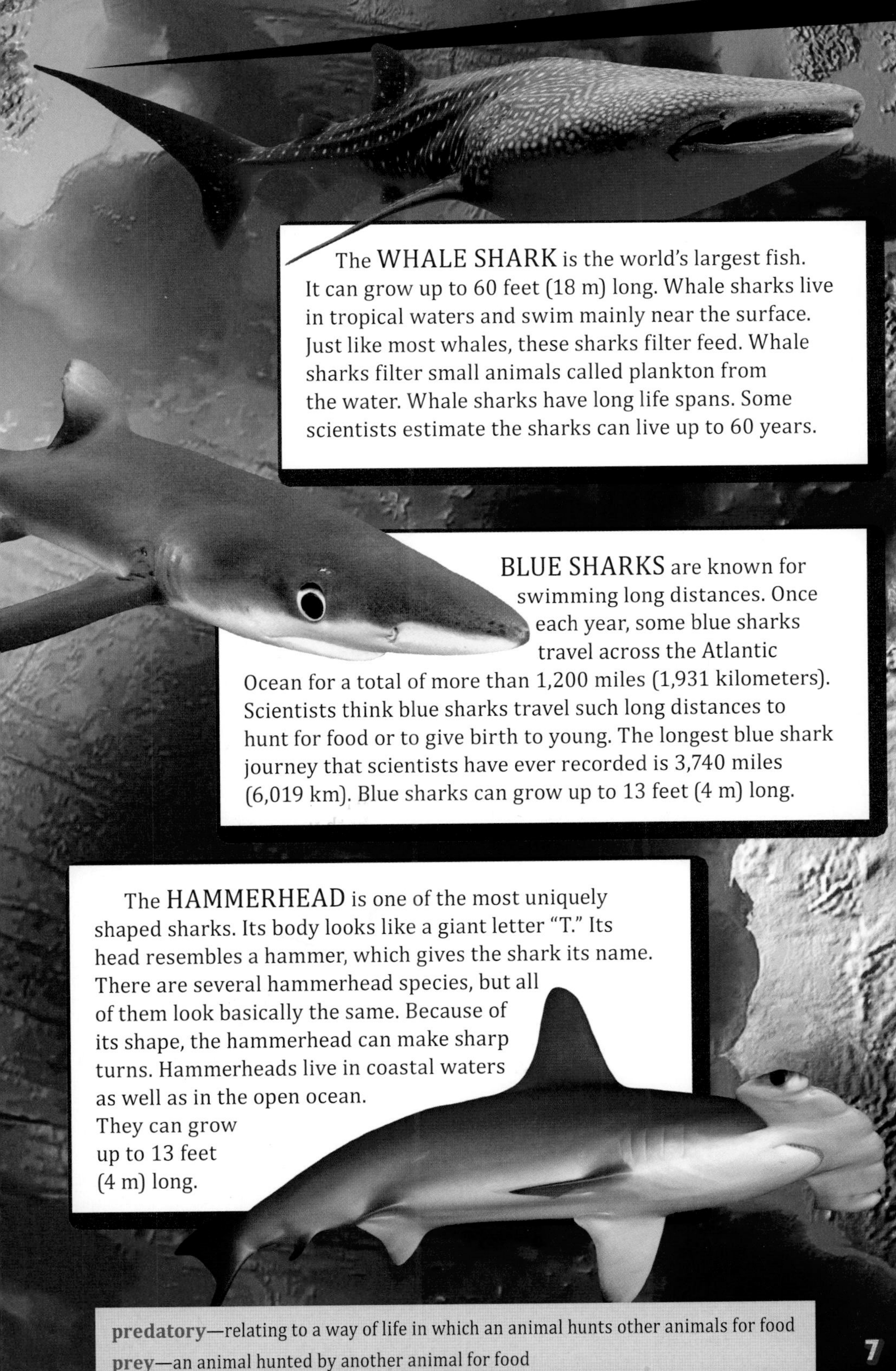

The **WHALE SHARK** is the world's largest fish. It can grow up to 60 feet (18 m) long. Whale sharks live in tropical waters and swim mainly near the surface. Just like most whales, these sharks filter feed. Whale sharks filter small animals called plankton from the water. Whale sharks have long life spans. Some scientists estimate the sharks can live up to 60 years.

BLUE SHARKS are known for swimming long distances. Once each year, some blue sharks travel across the Atlantic Ocean for a total of more than 1,200 miles (1,931 kilometers). Scientists think blue sharks travel such long distances to hunt for food or to give birth to young. The longest blue shark journey that scientists have ever recorded is 3,740 miles (6,019 km). Blue sharks can grow up to 13 feet (4 m) long.

The **HAMMERHEAD** is one of the most uniquely shaped sharks. Its body looks like a giant letter "T." Its head resembles a hammer, which gives the shark its name. There are several hammerhead species, but all of them look basically the same. Because of its shape, the hammerhead can make sharp turns. Hammerheads live in coastal waters as well as in the open ocean. They can grow up to 13 feet (4 m) long.

predatory—relating to a way of life in which an animal hunts other animals for food

prey—an animal hunted by another animal for food

A Prehistoric Beast

Scientists believe that sharks have been swimming in Earth's oceans for 400 million years. Over this time, sharks have changed very little. Divers who swim with great whites often say they feel like they've just stepped back—or swam back—in time. That's because great whites look very similar to their prehistoric ancestors, the megalodons.

great white

20 ft. (6 m)

Fact:

Sharks can replace a lost tooth in about 24 hours. They go through thousands of teeth in a lifetime.

The megalodon was a giant shark that lived more than 2 million years ago. Size is what sets great whites and megalodons apart. Megalodons were about three times as big as great whites—about as long as a city bus. A megalodon's teeth were massive. Just one megalodon tooth could cover the entire palm of an adult man's hand. And the open jaws of a megalodon were so big that a whole group of people could have stood inside of them!

megalodon

50 ft. (15 m)

reconstructed megalodon jaws

great white jaws

AT HOME IN THE OCEAN

Sharks are considered fish because they have backbones, live in water, breathe through gills, and have scales. But unlike other fish, shark skeletons are made of **cartilage** instead of bone. Every part of a shark's body is equipped perfectly for its life in the ocean.

A shark has an inner ear on each side of its head. Scientists believe that sharks can hear sounds from more than 800 feet (244 m) away. Experts think sound may be the first sense a shark uses to find prey.

The senses of a predatory shark keep it at the top of the ocean's food chain.

Sharks rely heavily on their sense of taste. They generally bite prey to find out what it is. If the shark doesn't like the taste, it usually rejects the prey and moves on. This behavior is known as a shark's "exploratory" bite.

Sharks are like the bloodhounds of the ocean. A very large part of a shark's brain is dedicated to smelling. Scientists think using the sense of smell could account for as much as one-third of the brain.

Predatory sharks have very good eyesight. In clear water, they can locate prey that is more than 50 feet (15 m) away. Sharks have special night vision. The eyes reflect light back through the retina twice instead of only once. This ability allows the sharks to see more clearly at night. Sharks can also change the size of their pupils to let in different amounts of light.

Fact:

A great white can detect a single drop of blood in 25 gallons (95 liters) of water.

cartilage—the strong, bendable material that forms some body parts on humans and animals

Sharks have a series of canals under their skin filled with fluid. These canals make up a shark's lateral line. The lateral line helps sharks sense movement in the surrounding water.

What's for Dinner?

All sharks are meat-eaters, but the type of animals they eat varies. Some sharks eat large animals, such as squid, turtles, dolphins, seals, and stingrays. Other sharks eat smaller animals, such as mollusks. Both of these types of sharks are predators because they actively hunt for food.

However, not all sharks are active hunters. Some sharks are filter feeders. These sharks swim with their mouths open. The water brings in small ocean animals called plankton. The water flows into the shark's mouth and out its gills. When the water goes out, the tiny animals are filtered through filtering pads or gill rakers. The food is then left behind for the shark to eat.

Chapter 2

IS THERE DANGER IN THE SEA?

Trio of Danger

A shark's life is simple. It grows, mates, and produces offspring. It needs food in order to do that. Great whites, tiger sharks, and bull sharks are the top hunters in the world of sharks. They often go after large animals, such as sea turtles and seals. They usually speed up underneath prey and attack from below. This element of surprise helps the shark get its dinner. Unfortunately, great white, tiger, and bull sharks are also responsible for most shark attacks on humans. They attack people the same way they attack any other prey, from underneath.

tiger shark

bull shark

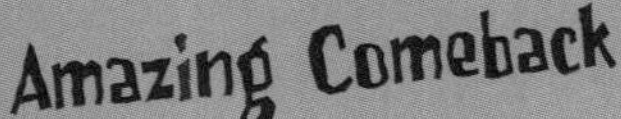

Amazing Comeback

Bethany Hamilton is a competitive surfer from the island of Kauai, Hawaii. When she was 13 years old, she was attacked by a 14-foot (4-m) tiger shark while surfing. She lost her left arm in the attack.

This experience would have kept many people out of the water. But not Bethany. She knew that what happened to her that day was just a freak accident. Bethany continues surfing in professional competitions around the world. A Hollywood movie was made about her story in 2011.

Scientists believe a shark may sense its prey by hearing it, smelling it, or feeling the prey's vibrations. They believe sharks attack humans by mistake. For example, if a shark saw a silhouette of a person on a surfboard, it may think the surfer is prey it normally hunts. The shark wouldn't know its mistake until after it had already taken its exploratory bite.

great white

Great White Attack!

In 1963 Rodney Fox suffered some of the most severe injuries ever recorded from a shark attack. He was competing in a spearfishing competition in his home state of South Australia. Rodney was an expert spearfisher and was defending his title that day.

Rodney was swimming about 65 feet (20 meters) below the surface of the water. Just as he reached back with his arm to spear a fish, he felt a sharp pain in his side. He looked back and saw the eyes of a great white. The giant shark had the entire left side of Rodney's body firmly in its jaws. Rodney was able to break free of the dagger-sharp teeth and make it to safety. But his wounds were severe. Every rib in his chest had been broken. He had deep puncture wounds on the upper half of his body, and his lung was punctured.

Rodney Fox's shark attack scars

Rodney had nearly lost his life, but he didn't let that affect his love of the ocean. He started a shark diving tour company to take people on shark dives in Australia. He even developed the first underwater shark cage so people could view great whites safely. Shark diving tour operators around the world use variations of this shark cage today.

Possible Spearfishing Dangers

Surfers are at risk of shark attacks because they can be mistaken as prey by sharks. Spearfishers may be at risk for other reasons. When a spearfisher stabs a fish, the fish releases blood in the water. Sharks are attracted to blood, so they will naturally come to the area. When the shark goes after the fish, the spearfisher could get in the way. Or the shark might take an exploratory bite of someone who is spearfishing.

Fact:

The waters off the coast of Western Australia are some of the deadliest for shark attacks. In 2011 three people were killed in the area. No other place in the world had as many deadly shark attacks that year.

Dangerous, but Rare

Although shark attacks like the ones on Bethany Hamilton and Rodney Fox are life-threatening, they are very rare. On average, sharks attack 50 to 70 people around the world each year. Of that number, an average of six attacks are fatal.

In 2000, 89 people around the world were attacked by sharks. That was the highest number ever recorded in a one-year period. Of those people, 11 died from the attacks. Only one of these fatal attacks happened in waters off the U.S. coast.

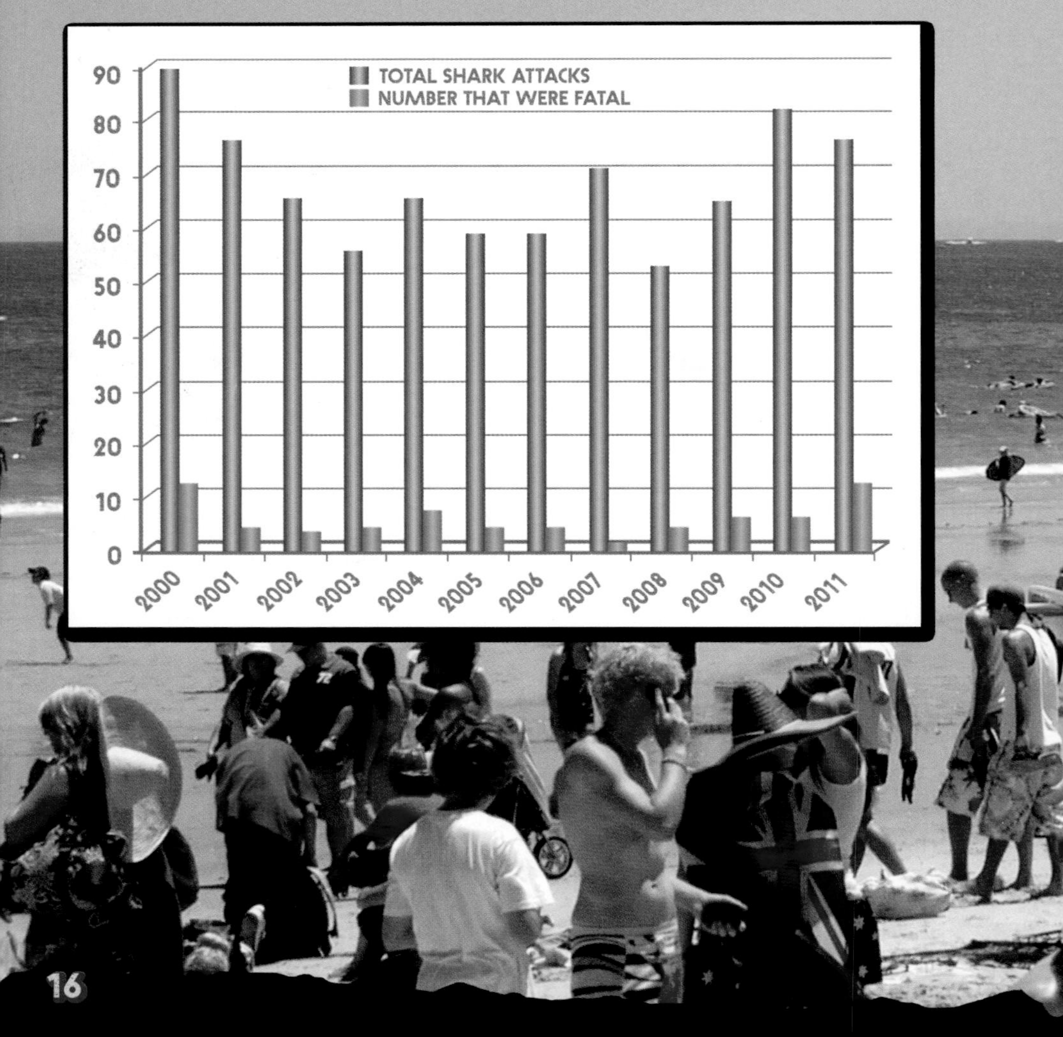

To put the rarity of shark attacks in perspective, consider these other statistics from the United States in 2000:

- 51 people were killed by lightning strikes
- 158 people died from heat exhaustion
- 41 people died because of winter storms

Q & A WITH SHARK EXPERT MARK ADDISON

QUESTION: If someone was afraid of getting into the ocean because of sharks, what would you say to calm his or her fears?

ANSWER: ... It is always sensible to swim at a beach with lifeguards. You should also make sure the water is clear and not murky. And you should ask if there has been any extraordinary **baitfish** activity in the area. You should ask if people have been catching a great deal of fish in the area recently. If so, sharks may be more likely to hunt in the area. Outside of these questions ... you must enjoy your swimming experience.

Fact:

Experts say people should not wear jewelry while swimming in the ocean. They say that jewelry is shiny like fish scales, and it may attract sharks.

baitfish—small fish that attract and are a food source for larger fish

Chapter 3

SIDE-BY-SIDE WITH SHARKS

Why Swim with Sharks?

People choose to dive into the ocean and swim near toothy sharks for many reasons. Here are just a few.

Learning About Nature

Many divers love what the underwater world has to offer. They enjoy looking at the plants and animals that live there. It is so different from what is on land that it's almost like another planet. To many divers, the best way to learn about nature is by exploring it firsthand.

Extreme Vacations

Some people like to have extreme adventures. These people skydive. They scale steep cliffs and try to reach the highest peaks. And some of these thrill seekers dive into the deep blue with sharks. Every year thousands of people go shark diving on their vacations. They see all kinds of sharks, including tiger sharks, great whites, hammerheads, and nurse sharks.

Relaxation

It might seem impossible to be relaxed while in the water with a shark. But many experienced divers say they dive with sharks to unwind. They say the ocean is a peaceful place where sounds are muted and colors are vibrant. Some animals, such as dolphins, create their own music as they click and sing. Other animals that live in coral reefs make a sound similar to sizzling bacon when they chomp on their dinners. Pebbles on the ocean floor clang as they bounce against one another with each wave. Fish of all sizes, including sharks, glide past you with ease as if you're part of the underwater world. Andy Brandy Casagrande IV explains, "I love how quiet and peaceful it is underwater. It's nothing like the scary music and sound effects that you hear and see on TV and in movies ... There's no traffic, no sirens, ... I just love it!"

Gathering Scientific Information

Many people who swim with sharks regularly are scientists. They believe that the best way to understand sharks is to interact with them in their natural environment. Taking videos of the animals helps scientists study their behavior. Shark expert Mark Addison currently has a large collection of blacktip and tiger shark videos and photographs. He says that the collection is important because it helps scientists learn how sharks behave in various situations. By learning more about sharks, experts can help ensure their survival.

Top Places to Swim with Sharks

FARALLON ISLANDS, CA:
GREAT WHITES

NEW ENGLAND COAST:
BLUE SHARKS

NC COAST:
TIGER SHARKS

CHANNEL ISLANDS, CA:
BLUE SHARKS,
HORN SHARKS,
ANGEL SHARKS

BAHAMAS:
HAMMERHEADS,
LEMON SHARKS,
REEF SHARKS,
TIGER SHARKS

GUADALUPE ISLAND, MEXICO:
GREAT WHITES

ISLA MUJERES, MEXICO:
WHALE SHARKS

COCOS ISLAND, COSTA RICA:
SCALLOPED HAMMERHEADS,
WHITETIP REEF SHARKS

GALAPAGOS ISLANDS, ECUADOR:
SCALLOPED HAMMERHEADS

Sharks can be found all around the world.
Here are some top places to swim with them.

PALAU ISLAND, PALAU SHARK SANCTUARY:
GRAY REEF SHARKS,
BLACKTIP SHARKS,
WHITETIP SHARKS,
OTHER SPECIES

MALDIVES, INDIA:
SCALLOPED HAMMERHEADS,
WHALE SHARKS,
ZEBRA SHARKS,
NURSE SHARKS,
SNAGGLETOOTH SHARKS,
OTHER SPECIES

GREAT BARRIER REEF, AUSTRALIA:
BLACKTIP REEF SHARKS,
CARPET SHARKS

SOUTH AFRICA:
GREAT WHITES,
TIGER SHARKS,
BULL SHARKS,
COPPER SHARKS

Shark Scientists

Many shark scientists have college degrees in **biology**, marine science, zoology, or oceanography. They usually study at universities that are close to the ocean. These locations allow the scientists to easily do work in the **field**.

Greg Skomal is a shark scientist and marine biologist who lives in Massachusetts. In a recent magazine article, he admitted that when he was a kid he thought that sharks were well studied and that there was no demand for shark scientists. But even today, there is a great need for shark scientists. Very little is known about these animals. Of the nearly 400 shark species, only about 100 have been studied.

Although many scientists who study sharks have a science degree, some shark experts have not attended universities. This fact doesn't mean they have less knowledge about sharks, though. Several of these experts grew up in families that made their living on the water. This background introduced them to sharks and other ocean life at an early age. Their years of hands-on experience with sharks give them valuable information.

a diver near a shark in the Bahamas

People study sharks for many reasons, including:

to protect sharks.

Sharks are important members of the ocean's ecosystem. Without them, the oceans will suffer. Other plants and animals will die out. Sharks keep ocean life balanced. Learning about sharks helps people ensure the animals' survival.

to protect people.

When people learn about sharks, they can understand how to keep people in the oceans safer.

to learn more about biology.

Studying sharks helps people learn more about animal behavior, the oceans, and the planet. Much of the ocean and ocean life remains unstudied. According to the National Oceanic and Atmospheric Administration (NOAA), about 95 percent of the ocean remains unexplored by people.

The Nitty-Gritty of Shark Research

If you think becoming a shark scientist is all about thrills, think again. Shark scientists often spend much more time indoors in their labs than they do in the ocean. When they do go out for field work, they have a lot of other issues to deal with. Sometimes the weather is not ideal. Sometimes their equipment won't work. Sometimes they don't see any sharks for days at a time. Shark research takes hard work, patience, and years of dedication.

biology—the study of plant and animal life

field—a type of study that involves firsthand observations outside of a laboratory

ecosystem—a group of animals and plants that work together with their surroundings

Gearing Up

Professional shark divers need different equipment depending on the species of shark they want to see. Shark diver and underwater photographer Mark Rackley says he always uses scuba gear to dive into Seattle's Puget Sound to see sixgill sharks. These sharks come out only at night and live on the bottom of the ocean. But when he dives with sharks in Florida or the Bahamas, he often dives without scuba gear by free diving.

scuba gear

fins

Wet suits keep divers warm in cold water.

Fins help divers travel quickly from place to place.

Scuba gear allows divers to breathe underwater. It includes an air tank, mask, breathing device, an air gauge, and a dive computer. The air gauge tells a diver how much air is left in the tank. The dive computer tracks the diver's depth, the diver's time spent in the water, and other information.

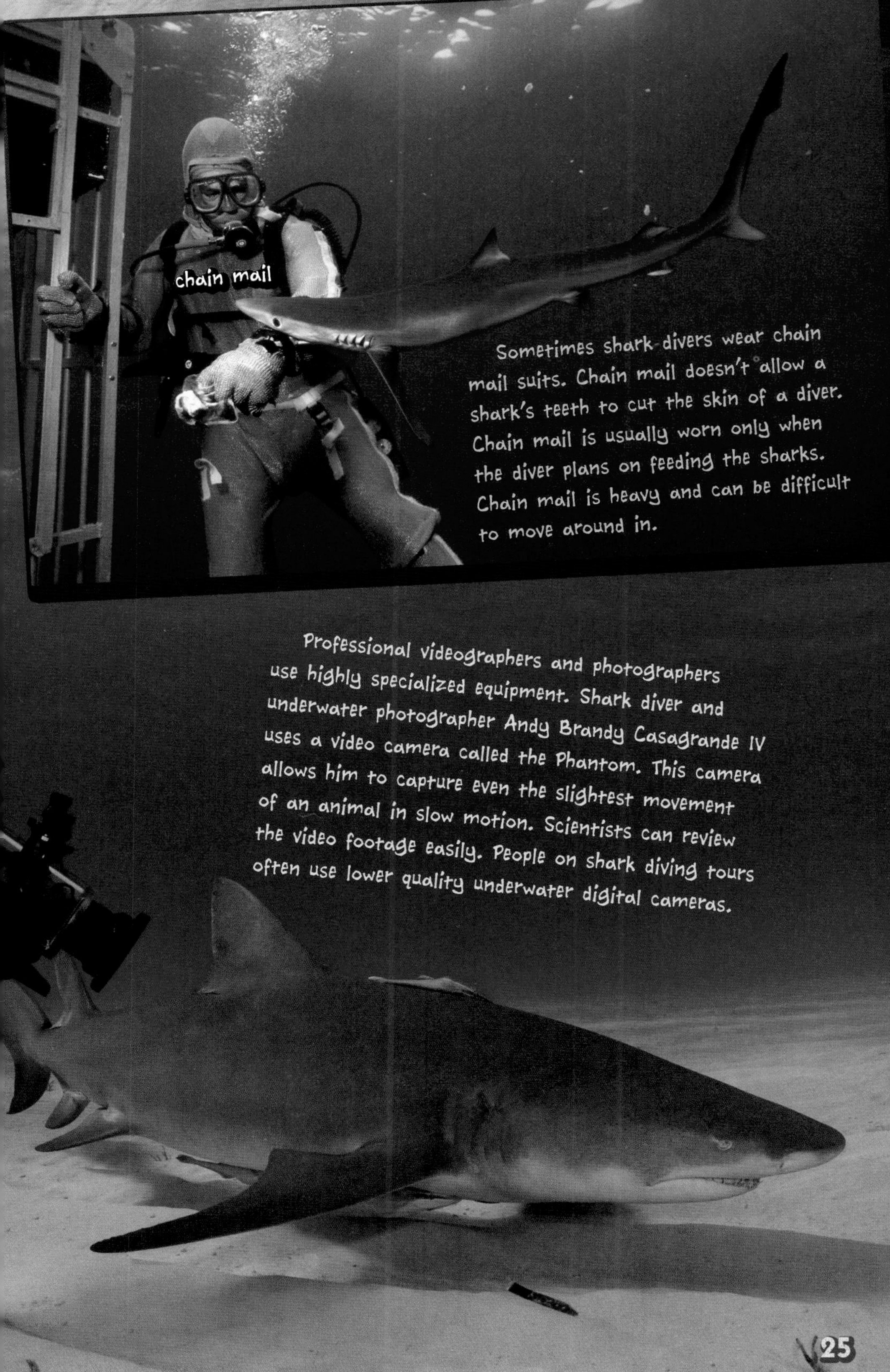

Sometimes shark divers wear chain mail suits. Chain mail doesn't allow a shark's teeth to cut the skin of a diver. Chain mail is usually worn only when the diver plans on feeding the sharks. Chain mail is heavy and can be difficult to move around in.

Professional videographers and photographers use highly specialized equipment. Shark diver and underwater photographer Andy Brandy Casagrande IV uses a video camera called the Phantom. This camera allows him to capture even the slightest movement of an animal in slow motion. Scientists can review the video footage easily. People on shark diving tours often use lower quality underwater digital cameras.

Free Diving

a free diver
with a whale shark

Free divers swim in wet suits with only a snorkel, mask, and fins. Instead of taking along oxygen tanks, they hold their breath. Free divers can hold their breath for a very long time. Free diver Mark Rackley says, "I am able to hold my breath for five and a half minutes. I am able to free dive on one breath to about 150 feet (46 m), which takes about two and a half minutes to complete."

Why do divers go into the deep ocean without any way to get air? According to the experts, it allows them to get very close to sharks. Scuba gear produces bubbles that can scare away sharks. Without scuba gear, the divers can get a better understanding of the animals' natural behavior.

Fact:

According to experts, free diving works especially well with hammerhead sharks.

TRACKING SHARKS

Many scientists want to find out what sharks do far away from prying human eyes. They want to know about sharks' **migration** patterns. They wonder where the animals' nursery areas are located and how sharks behave with one another. They wonder if there are areas where sharks routinely gather. Scientists are able to find out some of these things through shark tagging. Tags are usually placed on a shark's dorsal fin or at the top of its back.

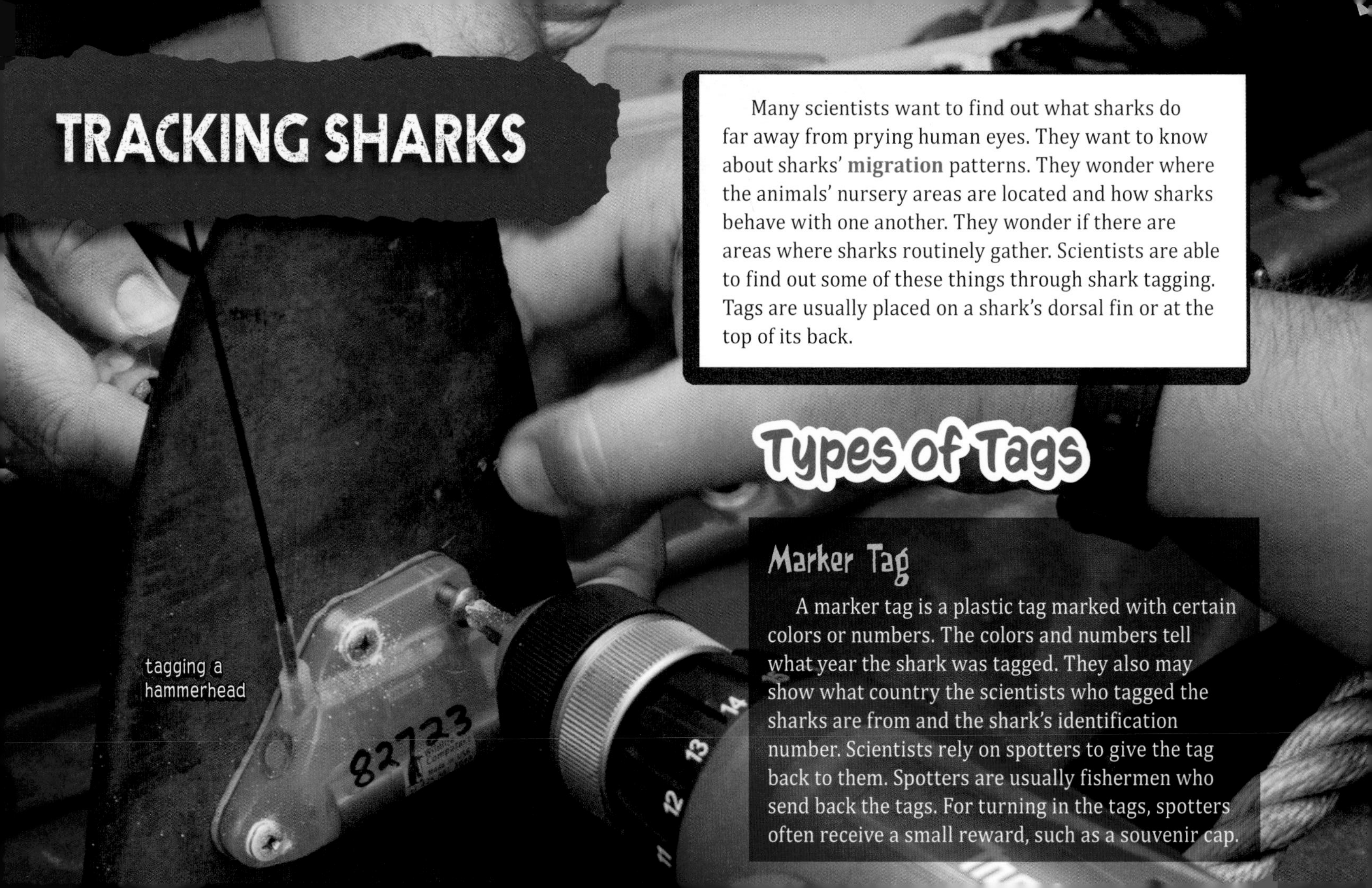

tagging a hammerhead

Types of Tags

Marker Tag

A marker tag is a plastic tag marked with certain colors or numbers. The colors and numbers tell what year the shark was tagged. They also may show what country the scientists who tagged the sharks are from and the shark's identification number. Scientists rely on spotters to give the tag back to them. Spotters are usually fishermen who send back the tags. For turning in the tags, spotters often receive a small reward, such as a souvenir cap.

Acoustic Tag

Acoustic tags send out sounds that are picked up by receivers. These tags are most often used for sharks that swim in a small area, such as a lagoon. They may also be used to follow a shark from a small boat. By using these tags, scientists can track the movement of sharks.

Acoustic tags transmit a unique code that can be detected by listening stations set on the bottom of the ocean. These stations record the date and time a tagged animal is present in the area. Sensors on acoustic tags can also transmit data including swimming depth, swimming speed, and water temperature.

Fact: The dorsal fins of sharks have few nerve endings. Scientists attach tags there so the sharks feel as little pain as possible.

Satellite Pop-Up Tag

Scientists attach satellite pop-up tags to sharks for a certain length of time. The tags record specific information, such as water depth and temperature. Then on a certain pre-programmed day, the tag releases itself from the shark. The tag floats up to the ocean's surface and sends the data it gathered to scientists using satellites.

Satellite Location-Only Tag

These tags are strapped onto the top of the shark or attached to the dorsal fin. When a shark swims at the surface, the tag pops out of the water. When the tag breaks the surface, it sends location information back to scientists using satellites.

migration—the regular movement of an animal from one place to another; animals often migrate to find food

satellite—a spacecraft that circles the Earth; satellites gather and send information

The Tagging Process

Scientists tag a variety of sharks. Tagging techniques vary depending upon the type of shark being tagged.

TAGGING A WHALE SHARK

On a whale shark tagging mission, scientists generally free dive or scuba dive close to the sharks. They then:

1. take pictures of the shark's skin pattern. Each whale shark has a different skin pattern. Scientists can use the pictures to identify the shark later.
2. attach the tag at the base of the dorsal fin with a tagging tool, such as a harpoon or a spear gun.

tagging a whale shark

Fact:

Since 1962 National Marine Fisheries Service (NMFS) scientists have been tagging blue sharks and other shark species in the Atlantic Ocean. The organization has tagged more than 52 different shark species and more than 100,000 individual sharks.

TAGGING A GREAT WHITE SHARK

Tagging the more toothy great white is a little more difficult. That's because great whites are more aggressive. A great white might feel threatened and bite a diver trying to put a tag on its dorsal fin. Scientists generally tag great whites through one of two ways:

1. Scientists catch the great white on a hook and line. They then hoist the shark out of the water using a big sling. Out of the water, the shark is safer to be around. They then attach the tag.
2. Scientists lure the shark with **chum** close to the boat. They then use a harpoon or a spear gun to attach the tag to the dorsal fin.

tagging a great white

Q & A WITH SHARK EXPERT CHRIS FALLOWS

QUESTION: How does tagging sharks help scientists?

ANSWER: If done sensitively and responsibly, it can help us learn a lot about shark movement, growth, and social interaction. That said, sharks should not just be tagged for the sake of some scientist doing a project. It must be done to help us learn more about these creatures so we can help conserve them.

chum—food dropped into the water to lure sharks; chum is often made up of dead fish parts

What Tagging Tells Us

Satellite pop-up tags provide scientists with a variety of information. Every 30 seconds or less, the tag records data. It can record:

- water temperature
- tag depth
- the amount of light in the part of the ocean the shark is swimming
- how long the shark has stayed in certain places

As soon as scientists receive the data, they use the recorded ocean light levels to map the shark's travels. They can then make a model of the shark's journey on a computer.

basking shark

Fact:

In June 2010 researchers tagged the first basking shark in the Pacific Ocean. Scientists are studying basking sharks to help develop a plan to increase their numbers.

This diagram shows an overview of what scientists might see when they plot out a shark's journey.

Shark tagging has provided scientists with a variety of information about sharks' travel patterns. In 2006 scientists found that one shark stayed four months in Hawaii before returning to California. In 2003 scientists tagged a group of great whites near South Africa. One female shark swam all the way from South Africa to Australia and back to South Africa. The total trip distance was 12,000 miles (19,312 km). She completed the journey in less than nine months.

Scientists sometimes study several sharks in the same area to see if they all follow the same travel patterns. This information helps the scientists see if sharks return to favorite places in a season. These could be places for feeding, socializing, mating, or giving birth.

SHARK SUBS

The DeepSee submersible was designed to help people explore deep-sea life. A driver and two passengers can fit inside. It currently dives near Costa Rica.

Some divers feel that the best way to view sharks in the wild is by using a small submarine. In the sub, divers don't need to worry about air bubbles scaring away the sharks. Divers can stay down much longer than they could by free diving. In a sub, divers can also follow sharks into deeper areas.

Several manufacturers have designed mini subs for shark observation. One is used on dives in the Caribbean Sea. Three people can ride inside this sub and be transported 3,000 feet (914 m) below the surface. Through an observation window, the passengers can see animals on the ocean floor, including sixgill sharks.

Ocean explorer Fabien Cousteau designed a sub in 2004 that looked like a great white shark. Cousteau wanted to get close to great whites in a vehicle that looked exactly like them. That way, the sharks wouldn't get scared off. Cousteau wanted to know what sharks do when they think no one is watching them.

Only one diver could fit inside Cousteau's steel sub. A special skin stretched over the steel to make it feel like a real shark. The sub cost more than $100,000 to build.

When Cousteau used the sub, he was impressed with what he observed. The sharks seemed to accept the sub as one of their own. A few even approached the sub with their mouths open and puffed out their gills in a form of communication.

Fact:

Cousteau's sub was designed to move at the cruising speed of a great white.

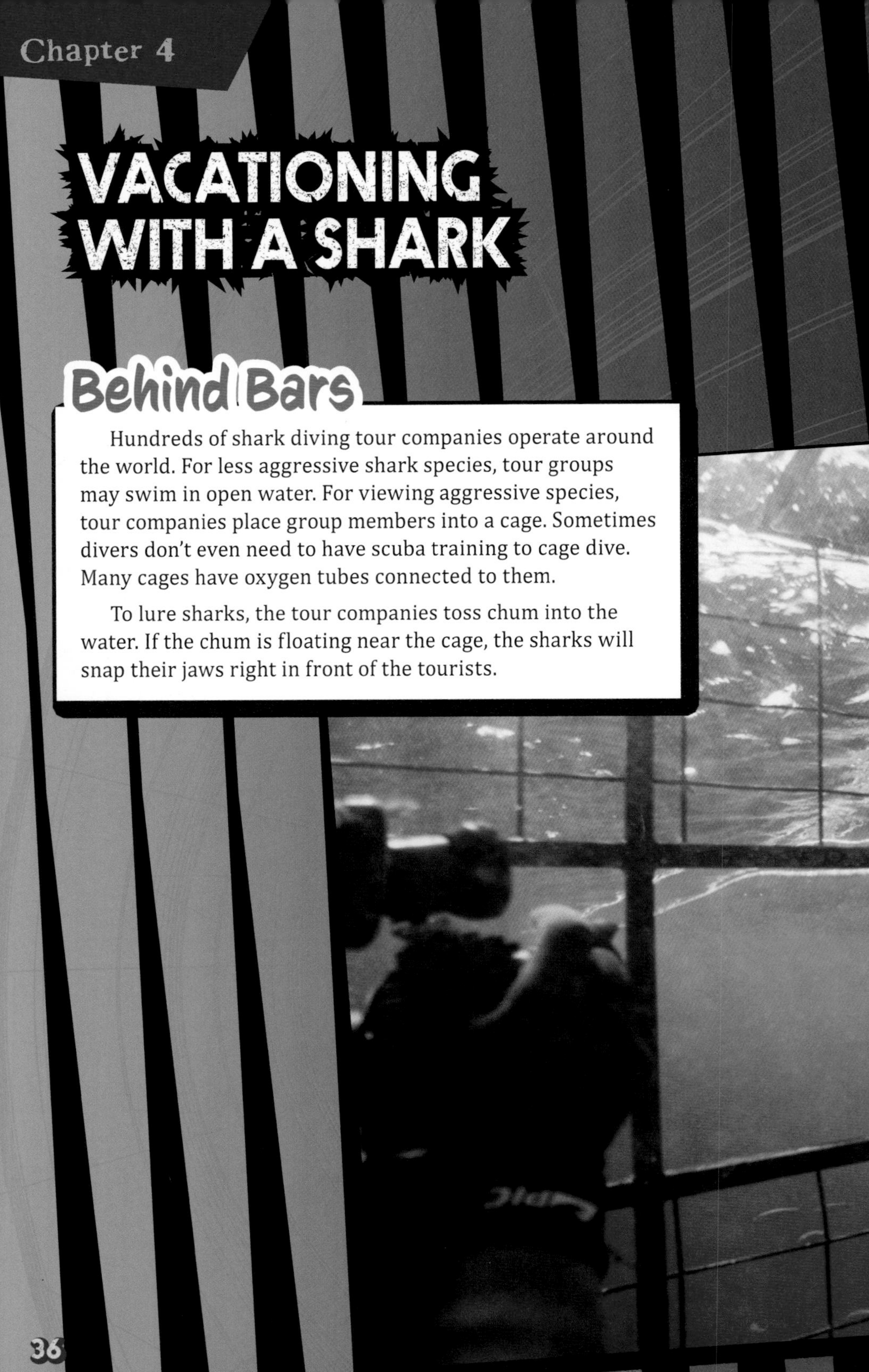

Chapter 4

VACATIONING WITH A SHARK

Behind Bars

Hundreds of shark diving tour companies operate around the world. For less aggressive shark species, tour groups may swim in open water. For viewing aggressive species, tour companies place group members into a cage. Sometimes divers don't even need to have scuba training to cage dive. Many cages have oxygen tubes connected to them.

To lure sharks, the tour companies toss chum into the water. If the chum is floating near the cage, the sharks will snap their jaws right in front of the tourists.

Cages are a great way to keep divers on tours safe. One disadvantage is that they don't allow people to see sharks' natural behavior. Sharks aren't used to eating chum, so they act differently around it. Shark expert Chris Fallows explains, "If I have a choice I will always dive outside of a cage as it is terrific to be with the sharks in their world ... Having said that, if conditions are not right I always respect that they are predators and as such I will use a cage."

Tourism Issues

Going on a tour group can be a great way to see sharks up close. But there are a lot of differing opinions surrounding shark diving tourism. Here are some pros and cons that people point out about shark diving tour groups.

PROS

Shark tourism educates people about sharks. After people see sharks in the wild, they often have a better opinion of the creatures. As a result, people are more likely to see the value in protecting these animals.

Shark tourism saves the lives of sharks. Instead of hunting sharks for their meat, people are trying to locate sharks for tourists. Locals still make money from the sharks, and the sharks' lives are not threatened.

Shark tourism provides jobs. In some countries, shark tourism provides thousands of jobs. A study in 2010 showed that hundreds of people in the Canary Islands had jobs in shark tourism. Shark diving tourists bring millions of dollars to the Canary Islands every year. Shark tourism is a huge money maker for many small countries throughout the world that have few other sources of income.

CONS

Shark tourism may increase the danger for surfers and ocean swimmers. Shark tour companies often use chum to attract sharks to boats and cages. Some people fear sharks are starting to associate food with people and boats. People have known for years that they shouldn't feed wild land animals. Feeding the animals can make them more aggressive toward humans. If this idea is true on land, it's probably true underwater too.

Shark diving operators also often take their tour groups near coastlines. When they toss chum into the water, they attract sharks. These areas haven't necessarily been feeding grounds for the sharks before. But the chum teaches sharks that they can come to these places to find food. More sharks near coastlines could lead to more attacks on people.

Some experts believe that changing sharks' natural behavior may lead to health problems for the animals. For example, sharks may become used to being fed by people in areas where tourism is common. The sharks may travel to these areas and wait to be fed. This behavior could lead to the sharks mating with relatives because the sharks no longer travel to find food and mates. Inbred animals are at risk for health problems.

Chapter 5

SHARKS IN DANGER

Humans are a greater threat to sharks than sharks are to people. Every year humans around the world hunt and kill more than 40 million sharks. Most of these sharks are killed for their dorsal fins to make shark fin soup. Because of this overhunting, sharks are considered one of the most threatened animals on Earth.

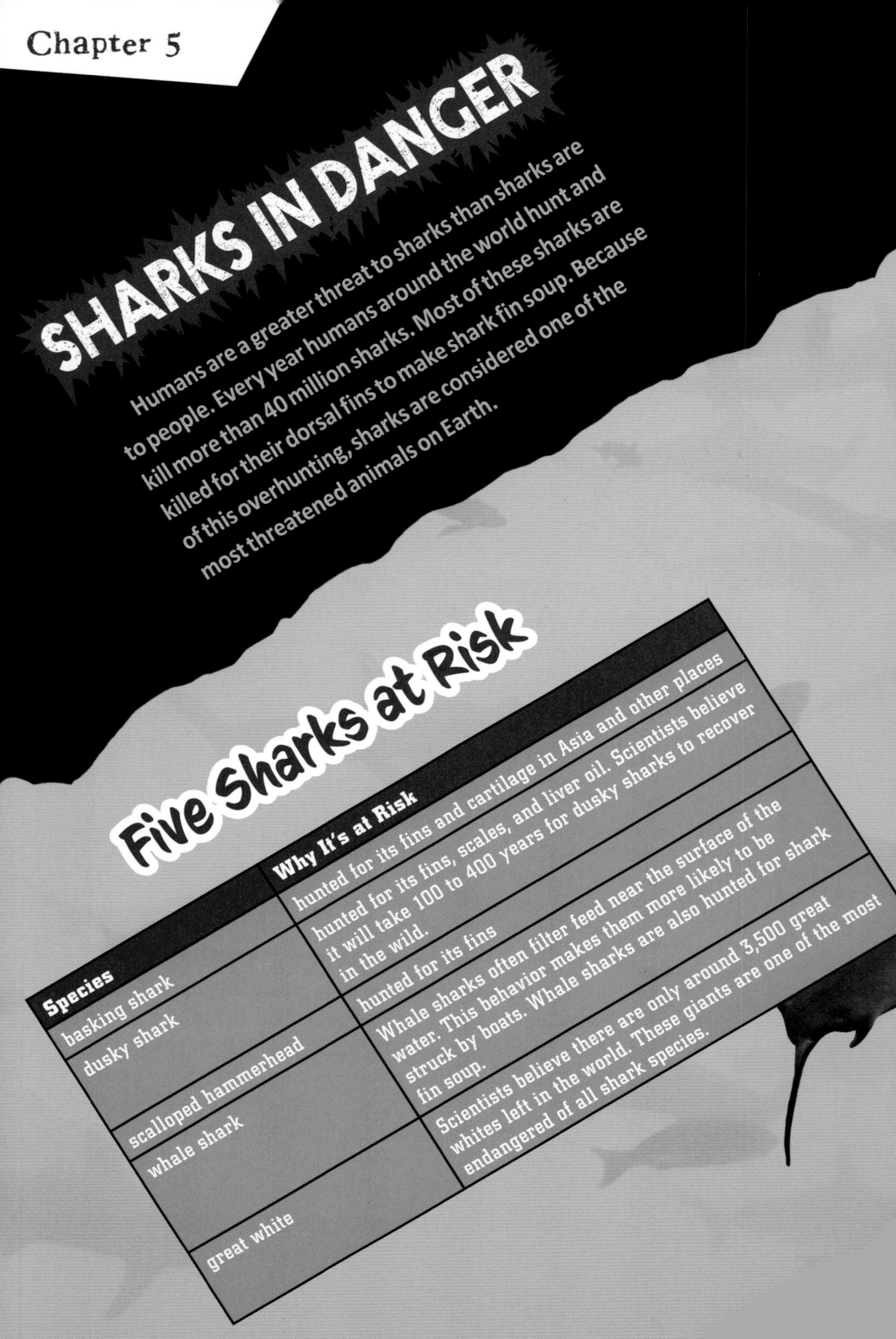

Five Sharks at Risk

Species	Why It's at Risk
basking shark	hunted for its fins and cartilage in Asia and other places
dusky shark	hunted for its fins, scales, and liver oil. Scientists believe it will take 100 to 400 years for dusky sharks to recover in the wild.
scalloped hammerhead	hunted for its fins
whale shark	Whale sharks often filter feed near the surface of the water. This behavior makes them more likely to be struck by boats. Whale sharks are also hunted for shark fin soup.
great white	Scientists believe there are only around 3,500 great whites left in the world. These giants are one of the most endangered of all shark species.

Protecting the Wild

Overfishing is the greatest threat to sharks. Some countries have passed laws to ban shark fishing and protect sharks. The tiny nation of Palau, Micronesia, in the Pacific Ocean was the first country to set up a shark sanctuary. An area about the size of France has been set aside for shark preservation. No hunting is allowed in the sanctuary's borders. Yet people can come to swim and dive with them. The Maldives near India has also created a shark sanctuary. More than 30 protected shark species surround the Maldives. Several shark dive tour companies operate in this area.

Conservation Efforts

Some conservation projects focus on the angel shark. Angel sharks often get caught in fishing nets and lines.

Recognizing that sharks need protection, some groups are working to help the animals. In 2003 the shark tourism company Shark Diver began a shark research program near Guadalupe Island, Mexico, to study great whites. Since then, Shark Diver has worked to promote shark conservation in the shark tourism industry. The company also encourages marinas around the world to ban sharks from being killed and landed at their locations.

The Wildlife Conservation Society works to protect ocean habitats and animals, including sharks. The coral reefs in the western Indian Ocean near Africa is one place the group is helping to conserve. This area is a habitat for 13 shark species.

Other groups persuade lawmakers to ban practices such as shark finning. Shark finning is the act of removing a shark's fin and leaving the shark to die.

Some marinas participate in the Shark-Free Marina Initiative. Many of these marinas post signs stating that sharks cannot be brought to their locations. Other participating marinas post signs discouraging shark landing.

Fact:

In January 2011 U.S. President Barack Obama signed the Shark Conservation Act. This law requires all sharks to be landed at U.S. locations with their fins attached. The law was a big step forward for shark conservation.

INTO THE DEEP

What's it really like to dive into the deep blue with sharks? And what keeps shark divers motivated for their next dive? Here's what some divers had to say:

Mark Rackley:

My favorite part of swimming with sharks is when I get to interact with them. The very best part is when it is approachable enough for me to catch a ride on its dorsal fin and ride it through the ocean.

George Kourounis:

I've learned that they are such amazing creatures ... I will never, ever eat shark fin soup, the thought of so many of these precious creatures suffering and dying for such a wasteful practice makes me very upset. I want to show the world that we can share the seas with these animals and not have to fear or slaughter them. We can watch them and appreciate them and the value they bring to the ecosystems of the oceans.

Andy Brandy Casagrande IV:

My most memorable experience diving with sharks was when I took my guitar underwater outside of the cage to play my "Great White Shark" song to seven different great white sharks [off the coast of] Mexico. They seemed to like the music!

Diving with sharks offers a rare opportunity to see these animals up close. As more people understand sharks better, scientists hope that more of these prehistoric creatures will be saved.

Glossary

baitfish (BAYT-fish)—small fish that attract and are a food source for larger fish

biology (by-AH-luh-jee)—the study of plant and animal life

cartilage (KAHR-tuh-lij)—the strong, bendable material that forms some body parts on humans and animals

chum (CHUHM)—food dropped into the water to lure sharks; chum is often made up of dead fish parts

conservation (kon-sur-VAY-shuhn)—the protection of animals and plants

ecosystem (EE-koh-sis-tuhm)—a system of living and nonliving things in an environment

field (FEELD)—a type of study that involves firsthand observations outside of a laboratory

free dive (FREE DIVE)—to swim underwater without scuba equipment and while holding your breath

marina (muh-REE-nuh)—a small harbor where boats are docked

migration (mye-GRAY-shuhn)—the regular movement of animals, usually to find food

predatory (PRED-uh-tor-ee)—relating to a way of life in which an animal hunts other animals for food

prey (PRAY)—an animal hunted by another animal for food

satellite (SAT-uh-lite)—a spacecraft that circles the Earth; satellites gather and send information

species (SPEE-sheez)—a group of plants or animals that share common characteristics

tropical (TRAH-pi-kuhl)—having to do with the hot and wet areas near the equator

Read More

Doubilet, David, and Jennifer Hayes. *Face to Face with Sharks.* Washington, D.C.: National Geographic, 2009.

Marsico, Katie. *Sharks.* Nature's Children. New York: Children's Press, 2012.

Musgrave, Ruth. *National Geographic Kids Everything Sharks: All the Shark Facts, Photos, and Fun That You Can Sink Your Teeth Into!* Washington, D.C.: National Geographic, 2011.

Internet Sites

FactHound offers a safe, fun way to find Internet sites related to this book. All of the sites on FactHound have been researched by our staff.

Here's all you do:

Visit *www.facthound.com*

Type in this code: 9781429699853

Index